A Study from Genesis

Pursued

God's Relentless Love for YOU

Jenny Youngman, Contributor

JENNIFER COWART

Abingdon Women | Nashville

Pursued
God's Relentless Love for YOU
Leader Guide

Copyright © 2021 Abingdon Press
All rights reserved.

ISBN 978-1-7910-1477-3

MANUFACTURED IN THE UNITED STATES OF AMERICA

Contents

About the Author

Jennifer Cowart is the executive and teaching pastor at Harvest Church in Warner Robins, Georgia, which she and her husband, Jim, began in 2001. With degrees in Christian education, counseling, and business, Jen oversees a wide variety of ministries and enjoys doing life and ministry with others. As a gifted Bible teacher, Jen brings biblical truth to life through humor, authenticity, and everyday application. She is the author of three women's Bible studies (*Pursued, Fierce,* and *Messy People*) and several small group studies coauthored with her husband, Jim, including *Grounded in Prayer* and *Living the Five.* They love doing life with their kids, Alyssa, Josh, and Andrew.

Follow Jen:

📷 jimandjennifercowart

f jimandjennifer.cowart

Website: jennifercowart.org or
          jimandjennifercowart.org
          (check here for event dates and booking information)

Introduction

Have you ever been pursued? If it was by law enforcement, a wild animal, or an unwelcome admirer, then I'm guessing it was a pretty bad experience. But if you have ever been pursued by someone who wants nothing but the best for you, then you know what real love is.

Friend, you are pursued by the God of the universe, and this is very good news! We all want to be loved. We long to be desired, *pursued*—whether by a special someone, our friends, or others in our lives. This longing for love and acceptance is the underlying story of your life and mine, and it's the overarching story we see throughout the Scriptures. Although there are many sub-stories in the Bible, there is really just one main theme: God's relentless love for us! From Genesis to Revelation, we see that God wants us to know Him, to love Him, and to live our lives in relationship with Him.

In *Pursued*, we will explore God's great love for us from Genesis to Revelation. We will see how God passionately pursues people who do not deserve His love, and we are those people! Like Cain, Abraham, Sarah, Rebekah, David, the woman caught in adultery, Peter, and so many others, we are the ones who have broken relationship with God. But He runs after us anyway to bring us home. Together we will study a great love story and discover that it is our story!

About the Participant Workbook

Before the first session, you will want to distribute copies of the participant workbook to the members of your group. Be sure to communicate that they are to complete the first week of readings *before* your first group session. For each week there are five devotional lessons that include both Scripture study as well as reflection and prayer. The lessons are designed to lead women through a quiet time with God where they savor His Word and allow Him to speak to them. Encourage the women in your group to find a quiet place—maybe a favorite chair or a spot on the porch, weather permitting—where they can spend their devotional study time.

Each day the lesson follows the same format: Settle, Focus, Reflect, and Pray. On average the lessons can be completed in about twenty to thirty minutes—depending on how much time is spent in prayer. Completing these readings each week will prepare the women for the discussion and activities of the group session.

About This Leader Guide

As you gather each week with the members of your group, you will have the opportunity to watch a video, discuss and respond to what you're learning, and pray together. You will need access to a television and a DVD player with working remotes. Or, if you prefer, you may purchase streaming video files at www.Cokesbury.com, or you may access the videos for this study and other Abingdon Women Bible studies on AmplifyMedia.com through an individual or church membership.

Creating a warm and inviting atmosphere will help to make the women feel welcome. Although optional, you might consider providing snacks for your first meeting and inviting group members to rotate in bringing refreshments each week.

This leader guide and the DVD/video files will be your primary tools for leading each group session. In this book you will find outlines for six group sessions, plus an introductory session, each formatted for either 60 or 90 minutes:

60-Minute Format

Leader Prep (Before the Session)	
Welcome and Opening Prayer	5 minutes
Icebreaker	5 minutes
Video	15–20 minutes
Group Discussion	25 minutes
Closing Prayer	5 minutes

90-Minute Format

Leader Prep (Before the Session)	
Welcome and Opening Prayer	5–10 minutes

Icebreaker	5 minutes
Video	15–20 minutes
Group Discussion	30–35 minutes
Deeper Conversation	15 minutes
Closing Prayer	5 minutes

As you can see, the 90-minute format is identical to the 60-minute format but has more time for welcoming/fellowship and group discussion, plus a deeper conversation exercise for small groups. Or your group might prefer to limit the welcoming time and extend the closing prayer time. Feel free to adapt or modify either format, as well as the individual segments and activities, in any way to meet the specific needs and preferences of your group.

Here is a brief overview of the elements included in both formats:

Leader Prep (Before the Session)

For your preparation prior to the group session, this section provides an overview of the week's Bible story and theme, the main point of the session, key Scriptures, and a list of materials and equipment needed. Be sure to review this section, as well as the session outline, to plan and prepare before the group meets. If you choose, you also may find it helpful to watch the video segment in advance.

Welcome and Opening Prayer (5–10 minutes, depending on session length)

To create a warm, welcoming environment as the women are gathering before the session begins, consider lighting one or more candles, providing coffee or other refreshments, or playing worship music, or all of these. (Bring an iPod, smartphone, or tablet and a portable speaker if desired.) Be sure to provide name tags if the women do not know one another or you have new participants in your group. Then, when you are ready to begin, pray the opening prayer that is provided or offer your own.

Icebreaker (5 minutes)

Use the icebreaker to briefly engage the women in the topic while helping them feel comfortable with one another.

Video (15–20 minutes)

Next, watch the week's video segment together. Be sure to direct participants to the Video Viewer Guide in the participant workbook, which they may complete as they watch the video. (Answers are provided on page 203 of the participant workbook and page 64 of this leader guide.)

Group Discussion (25–35 minutes, depending on session length)

After watching the video, choose from the questions provided to facilitate group discussion (questions are provided for both the video and the participant workbook). For the workbook portion, you may choose to read aloud the talking points—*which are excerpts from the participant workbook*—or express them in your own words; then use one or more of the questions that follow to guide your conversation.

Note that more material is provided than you will have time to include. Before the session, select what you want to cover, putting a check mark beside it in your book. Reflect on each question and make some notes in the margins to share during your discussion time. Page references are provided for those questions that relate to specific questions or activities in the participant workbook. For these questions, invite group members to turn in their workbooks to the pages indicated. Participants will need Bibles in order to look up various supplementary Scriptures.

Depending on the number of women in your group and the level of their participation, you may not have time to cover everything you have selected, and that is okay. Rather than attempting to bulldoze through, follow the Spirit's lead and be open to where the Spirit takes the conversation. Remember that your role is not to have all the answers but to encourage discussion and sharing.

Deeper Conversation (15 minutes)

If your group is meeting for 90 minutes, move next to this exercise for deeper sharing in small groups, dividing into groups of two or three. This is a time for women to share more intimately and build connections with one another. (Encourage the women to break into different groups each week.) Before the session, write the question or questions you want to discuss on a marker board or chart paper for all to see. Give a two-minute warning before time is up so that the groups may wrap up their discussion.

Closing Prayer (5 minutes)

Close by leading the group in prayer. Invite the women to briefly name prayer requests. To get things started, you might share a personal request of your own. As women share their requests, model for the group by writing each request in your participant workbook, indicating that you will remember to pray for them during the week.

As the study progresses, you might encourage members to participate in the Closing Prayer by praying out loud for one another and the requests given. Ask the women to volunteer to pray for specific requests, or have each woman pray for the woman on her right or left. Make sure name tags are visible so that group members do not feel awkward if they do not remember someone's name.

After the prayer, remind the women to pray for one another throughout the week.

Before You Begin

Friends, it took me many years to realize that God was pursuing me. I thought I had to pursue Him in order to find Him. What a relief to know that He was seeking me all along. The personal stories of the characters we will be studying reveal the same thing. God was running after them—just as He's running after you. No matter what you've done or not done, no matter how far you've drifted or how disconnected you've felt, you are loved. In fact, you are pursued!

Blessings, *dear friend,*

Jen

Basic
Leader Helps

Preparing for the Sessions

- Check out your meeting space before each group session. Make sure the room is ready. Do you have enough chairs? Do you have the equipment and supplies you need? (See the list of materials needed in each session outline.)
- Pray for your group and each group member by name. Ask God to work in the life of every woman in your group.
- Read and complete the week's readings in the participant workbook and review the session outline in the leader guide. Put a check mark beside the discussion questions you want to cover and make any notes in the margins that you want to share in your discussion time. If you want, you may also choose to view the video segment.

Leading the Sessions

- Personally greet each woman as she arrives. If desired, take attendance. (This will assist you in identifying members who have missed several sessions so that you may contact them and let them know they were missed.)
- At the start of each session, ask the women to turn off or silence their cell phones.
- Always start on time. Honor the efforts of those who are on time.
- Encourage everyone to participate fully, but don't put anyone on the spot. Invite the women to share as they are comfortable. Be prepared to offer a personal example or answer if no one else responds at first.
- Facilitate but don't dominate. Remember that if you talk most of the time, group members may tend to listen passively rather than to engage personally.
- Try not to interrupt, judge, or minimize anyone's comments or input.

- Remember that you are not expected to be the expert or have all the answers. Acknowledge that all of you are on this journey together, with the Holy Spirit as your leader and guide. If issues or questions arise that you don't feel equipped to answer or handle, talk with the pastor or a staff member at your church.
- Encourage good discussion, but don't be timid about calling time on a particular question and moving ahead. Part of your responsibility is to keep the group on track. If you decide to spend extra time on a given question or activity, consider skipping or spending less time on another question or activity in order to stay on schedule.
- Try to end on time. If you are running over, give members the opportunity to leave if they need to. Then wrap up as quickly as you can.
- Be prepared for some women to want to hang out and talk at the end. If you need everyone to leave by a certain time, communicate this at the beginning of the session. If you are meeting in a church during regularly scheduled activities or have arranged for childcare, be sensitive to the agreed-upon ending time.
- Thank the women for coming, and let them know you're looking forward to seeing them next time.

Introductory Session

Note:
This session is designed to
be 60 minutes in length.

Leader Prep

Overview of the Session

This session is an opportunity to give an overview of the study, get to know one another and share hopes for the study, and handle some housekeeping details such as collecting information for a group roster (name, email address, primary phone number, and, if desired, mailing address), making decisions regarding childcare and refreshments, distributing or providing instructions for purchasing books, and praying together.

Note: Participants need to complete the devotional lessons for Week 1 prior to the session for Week 1.

Main Point

In *Pursued*, we will explore God's great love for us from Genesis to Revelation. We will see how God passionately pursues people who do not deserve His love, and we are those people! Like Cain, Abraham, Sarah, Rebekah, David, the woman caught in adultery, Peter, and so many others, we are the ones who have broken relationship with God. But He runs after us anyway to bring us home. Together we will study a great love story and discover that it is our story!

Key Scripture(s)

[10]As the rain and snow come down from heaven and stay upon the ground to water the earth, and cause the grain to grow and to produce seed for the farmer and bread for the hungry, [11]so also is my word. I send it out, and it always produces fruit. It shall accomplish all I want it to and prosper everywhere I send it.

(Isaiah 55:10-11, TLB)

What You Will Need

- *Pursued* DVD and DVD player, or equipment to stream the video online
- marker board or chart paper and markers
- stick-on name tags and markers (optional)
- iPod, smartphone, or tablet and portable speaker (optional)

Session Outline

Welcome and Opening Prayer (15 minutes)

To create a warm, welcoming environment as the women are gathering before the session begins, consider lighting one or more candles, providing coffee or other refreshments, or playing worship music, or all of these. (Bring an iPod, smartphone, or tablet and a portable speaker if desired.) Be sure to provide name tags if the women do not know one another or you have new participants in your group. Take time to introduce yourselves and fellowship for a while. Then, when you are ready to begin, pray the following prayer or offer your own:

Dear God, thank You for pursuing us. Thank You for Your Word that instructs us and illuminates Your truth. Thank You for community where we can study, learn, and grow in Your love and grace. Come and reveal Your heart to us as we seek You. We love You. Amen.

Icebreaker (10 minutes)

Go around the circle twice, inviting the women to share short, "popcorn" responses to the following questions each time:

- When have you been pursued by someone? Maybe a job recruiter, or a love interest?
- What do you think it means that God pursues you?

Introductory Comments (5 minutes)

- Read or summarize the content from the introduction in the Participant Workbook (pages 9-11), reviewing the focus and purpose of the study as well as the format.

Group Discussion (25 minutes)

- Read Isaiah 55:10-11. How has God's Word taken root in your life and produced fruit?
- Review the list of weekly topics—Pursued from the Very Beginning, Pursued through Growing Pains, Pursued in a Cycle of Obedience and Rebellion, Pursued and Rescued, Pursued in Our Unsavory Moments, and Pursued for the Sake of Others. What do you already know about the ways in which the Bible is a story of God pursuing us?
- What are your hopes for this study? What do you want to gain from it?

Closing Prayer (5 minutes)

Close the session by taking personal prayer requests from group members and leading the group in prayer. As you progress to later weeks in the study, you might encourage members to participate in the Closing Prayer by praying out loud for one another and the requests given.

Week 1

Pursued from the Very Beginning

CREATION

Leader Prep

Bible Story and Theme Overview

This week, we looked to the Creation story in Genesis to discover how God has pursued us from the very beginning. We saw perfection in the garden, then sin, then shame, then consequence, then mercy. We have seen how sin disrupted the perfection that God created for us. But, we also have seen that, as a loving Father, God continually creates a pathway back to Him—ultimately, not even sparing His own Son at the cross in order for us to live in unbroken fellowship with Him.

Main Point

The Creator of the universe pursues His creation with a relentless love. His goal, His joy, is that all would come to know and love Him as He knows and loves us.

Key Scripture(s)

¹In the beginning God created the heavens and the earth. ²The earth was formless and empty, and darkness covered the deep waters. And the Spirit of God was hovering over the surface of the waters.

³Then God said, "Let there be light," and there was light. ⁴And God saw that the light was good. Then he separated the light from the darkness. ⁵God called the light "day" and darkness "night."

And evening passed and morning came, marking the first day....

> *²⁷So God created human beings in his own image.*
> *In the image of God he created them;*
> *male and female he created them.*

²⁸Then God blessed them and said, "Be fruitful and multiply. Fill the earth and govern it. Reign over the fish in the sea, the birds in the sky, and all the animals that scurry along the ground."

²⁹Then God said, "Look! I have given you every seed-bearing plant throughout the earth and all the fruit trees for your food. ³⁰And I have given every green plant as food for all the wild animals, the birds in the sky, and the small animals that scurry along the ground—everything that has life." And that is what happened.

³¹Then God looked over all he had made, and he saw that it was very good!

(Genesis 1:1-5, 27-31)

What You Will Need

- *Pursued* DVD and DVD player, or equipment to stream the video online
- marker board or chart paper and markers
- stick-on name tags and markers (optional)
- iPod, smartphone, or tablet and portable speaker (optional)

Session Outline

Welcome and Opening Prayer (5–10 minutes, depending on session length)

To create a warm, welcoming environment as the women are gathering before the session begins, consider lighting one or more candles, providing coffee or other refreshments, or playing worship music, or all of these. (Bring an iPod, smartphone, or tablet and a portable speaker if desired.) Be sure to provide name tags if the women do not know one another or you have new participants in your group. Then, when you are ready to begin, pray the following prayer or offer your own:

Dear God, thank You for pursuing us from the very beginning. Thank You for looking at Your creation with eyes of love and the heart of a good father. Help us to open our hearts to what You have to show us as we gather with friends around Your Word. Amen.

Icebreaker (5 minutes)

Invite the women to share short, "popcorn" responses to the following question:

- What are some famous stories of pursuit that you can remember—maybe a famous car chase, literature romance, or a politician's road to power?

Video (15–20 minutes)

Play the Week 1 video segment. Invite participants to complete the Video Viewer Guide for Week 1 in the participant workbook as they watch (page 41).

Group Discussion (25–35 minutes, depending on session length)

Note: More material is provided than you will have time to include. Before the session, select what you want to cover, putting a check mark beside it in your book. Page references are provided for questions related to questions or activities in the participant workbook. For these questions, invite participants to share the answers they wrote in their books.

Video Discussion Questions

- Can you imagine this planet, everything about it, being healthy and in its right order—every relationship you have, including your relationship with God, being very good, excellent in every way? What would that look and feel like?
- What does it mean that we live with brokenness?
- How does the human tendency to do our own thing show up in the Bible? How does it keep us from flourishing?
- How have you known the passionate, pursuing love of God in your life?

Participant Workbook Discussion Questions

1. God's love not only endures the hard times but also pursues us in those times when we are distant. (Day 1, page 14)

   - Who are you willing to love, forgive, and fight for no matter what? (page 15)
   - How do you put that into practice? (page 15)
   - Read Genesis 1. According to verse 31, how did God describe all that He had made? (page 15)

2. We were created so that God could enjoy a relationship with us! He was not content to live without us, so He created our world and put us here so that He could live in relationship with us. . . . You were created to be loved by God. His plan since the beginning of time has been to adopt you into His family so that you and He can enjoy a pure and precious bond. (Day 1, page 16)

- Read Zephaniah 3:17. According to this verse, how does God show His delight in us? (page 16)
- Read Ephesians 1:5 and Colossians 1:16. What do these passages reveal to us about God's purpose for creation? (page 16)
- How do you see God's pursuit of us from beginning to end in Scripture?

3. Adam and Eve chose their will over God's, and that's called sin. Sin creates a wedge—a sense of separation—between us and God, and that, friend, is a very big deal. (Day 2, page 20)

- Read Genesis 3:1-7a. What happens in verse 7, and what emotion do Adam and Eve feel in response? (page 23)
- Would you say that humans have a tendency to downplay sin? Why do you think that is?
- Read Hosea 6:6 and Romans 6:23. What is the heart of God related to our sin? When and how have you experienced "death" because of sin? (page 20)

4. Only three chapters into the Bible, we see the great virus of sin infect the whole human race. I am a carrier of this disease, and so are you. Yet, as we will see, God has the antidote for sin. He pursues us as a great and compassionate physician offering the vaccine to all who will turn to Him. And He does this out of His overwhelming love for each of us. (Day 2, page 24)

- How have you seen moral decline in your lifetime? (page 22)
- Read Romans 3:23 and 1 John 1:8. Are there any among us without sin? How might we sometimes deceive ourselves regarding our own sin?
- Where does shame enter the Creation story (see again Genesis 3:7)? How have you known God to be an antidote to your sin and shame?

5. Perhaps, it is pride that keeps us from taking responsibility for our own sins and shortcomings. Perhaps, we would just rather live in denial. Or perhaps, it's just so much easier to recognize sin in someone else's life than it is to see it in our own. (Day 3, page 27)

- Read Genesis 3:11-17. Where do denial and blame enter the story?
- Why is it so easy to blame others or even blame God for our own sin?

- Read Matthew 7:3-5. What trap does Jesus describe in these verses? (page 28)
- Why is it easier to see the sin in other people's lives and miss our own struggles with sin?

6. Sin is like a cancer. It can grow and become part of the very fabric of our being. In fact, it doesn't take long at all to become very comfortable with our particular varieties of sin.... God stands ready to offer us forgiveness. Jesus's grace has already been extended to us, but it is not a cheap grace. It has come at a price—that of God's own Son. (Day 3, page 28)

- In what ways have you seen sin act as a cancer, poisoning lives, releationships, or even churches?
- Read Psalm 139:23-24. What is the prayer of David's heart? How might this prayer lead us to a life of flourishing?
- How is it that God loves us even when we are full of sin?

7. After their disobedience, Adam and Eve were driven from the garden of Eden. They had enjoyed precious times with their Creator. These were times of pure peace and joy, but that had been interrupted by a willful act of disobedience. They, like us, became convinced that they knew better than God what was best for them, and they made a choice against God's law. Those choices, known as sin, have consequences. (Day 4, page 32)

- Read Genesis 3:22-24. What was the shared consequence for Adam and Eve? (page 32)
- Read Isaiah 55:8-9. When have you struggled to give up your plan and embrace God's plan for your life? (page 33)
- What does it mean that God's ways are higher than our ways?

8. Though we don't deserve it, [God] continually pursues us. Even when we are hurting and distant, God stands ready to receive us when we turn to Him. It's often only in retrospect that we see how He has looked out for us and sought us out throughout our lives. (Day 4, page 34)

- As you look back on your life, in what ways can you see God guiding you, looking out for you, even when you were not looking for Him? (page 32)

- Looking back, can you see any evidence of God's love and mercy in that particular time or circumstance [when you struggled to give up your plan and embrace God's plan]? (page 33)
- Read Jeremiah 29:13. What is the promise for us in this verse?

9. God's creation is now born into a broken world that only vaguely resembles what God originally intended. But God's children, those who are adopted into His family, will experience that perfection one day in heaven. There is a distinction between God's creation and God's children. Everyone is a part of God's creation, but to be a child of God means being adopted into His family. That happens the moment we repent of our sins and receive Jesus, God's Son, as our Lord and Savior. At that moment, we are justified by our faith. (Day 5, page 37)

- Read John 1:12 and 1 John 3:1. What do these verses mean to you?
- Read 1 Corinthians 15:21-22. What does this verse promise those who belong to Christ?
- Read John 3:16-17. When was the first time you heard these verses? What have they meant to you on your journey with Jesus? What is the promise that we can hold on to when we have doubts about our belovedness or freedom from sin?

10. This week we have seen how sin disrupted the perfection that God created for us. But, we have also seen that, as a loving Father, God continually creates a pathway back to Him— ultimately, not even sparing His own Son at the cross in order for us to live in unbroken fellowship with Him. (Day 5, page 39)

- Read 1 Corinthians 15:21-22. What does this verse promise those who belong to Christ? (page 39)
- How would you describe "new life" in Jesus?

11. The Creator of the universe pursues His creation with a relentless love. His goal, His joy, is that all would come to know and love Him as He knows and loves us. (Day 5, pages 39–40)

- What thoughts or discoveries are sticking with you from this week's study?

Deeper Conversation (15 minutes, for a 90-minute session)

Divide into smaller groups of two or three for deeper conversation. (Encourage the women to break into different groups each week.) Before the session, write on a marker board or chart paper the question or questions you want the groups to discuss:

- Reflecting on the story of Creation, what would you say is the arc of the story?
- How is your own journey with God reflected in the Creation story?
- Discuss life in the garden before sin and after sin. Then, if you're comfortable, share a little about your life before Jesus and after Jesus.

Give a two-minute warning before time is up so that the groups may wrap up their discussion.

Closing Prayer (5 minutes)

Close the session by taking personal prayer requests from group members and leading the group in prayer. As you progress to later weeks in the study, you might encourage members to participate in the Closing Prayer by praying out loud for one another and the requests given.

Pursued through Growing Pains

PATRIARCHS AND MATRIARCHS OF THE FAITH

Leader Prep

Bible Story and Theme Overview

This week, we have seen how God chose to start His holy nation through imperfect people. Abraham, Isaac, and Jacob are known as the great patriarchs of the faith. Yet, they were all flawed. So were their wives and children. This is good news for us. We too are flawed. Our stories are messy, but God pursues us with a relentless love.

Main Point

God never wants to waste a hurt. He can turn your greatest suffering into your greatest ministry if you allow it

Key Scripture(s)

¹The Lord had said to Abram, "Leave your native country, your relatives, and your father's family, and go to the land that I will show you. ²I will make you into a great nation. I will bless you and make you famous, and you will be a blessing to others. ³I will bless those who bless you and curse those who treat you with contempt. All the families on earth will be blessed through you." . . .

⁷"I will confirm my covenant with you and your descendants after you, from generation to generation. This is the everlasting covenant: I will always be your God and the God of your descendants after you. ⁸And I will give you the entire land of Canaan, where you now live as a foreigner, to you and your descendants. It will be their possession forever, and I will be their God."

(Genesis 12:1-3; 17:7-8)

¹⁹This is the account of the family of Isaac, the son of Abraham. ²⁰When Isaac was forty years old, he married Rebekah. . . . ²¹Isaac pleaded with the Lord on behalf of his wife, because she was unable to have children. The Lord answered Isaac's prayer, and Rebekah became pregnant with twins.

(Genesis 25:19-21)

Get rid of all bitterness, rage and anger, brawling and slander, along with every form of malice.

(Ephesians 4:31 NIV)

You are a chosen people. You are royal priests, a holy nation, God's very own possession. As a result, you can show others the goodness of God, for he called you out of the darkness into his wonderful light.

(1 Peter 2:9)

We can rejoice, too, when we run into problems and trials, for we know that they help us develop endurance.

(Romans 5:3)

What You Will Need

- *Pursued* DVD and DVD player, or equipment to stream the video online
- marker board or chart paper and markers
- stick-on name tags and markers (optional)
- iPod, smartphone, or tablet and portable speaker (optional)

Session Outline

Welcome and Opening Prayer (5–10 minutes, depending on session length)

To create a warm, welcoming environment as the women are gathering before the session begins, consider lighting one or more candles, providing coffee or other refreshments, or playing worship music, or all of these. (Bring an iPod, smartphone, or tablet and a portable speaker if desired.) Be sure to provide name tags if the women do not know one another or you have new participants in your group. Then, when you are ready to begin, pray the following prayer or offer your own:

Dear God, thank You for never leaving us where we are. You meet us in our mess and promise to make all things good. You change us and shape us into who You made us to be. Speak to us as we study Your Word. Reveal to us Your pursuit of our hearts and help us to say yes to Your love. Amen.

Icebreaker (5 minutes)

Invite the women to share short, "popcorn" responses to the following question:

- Briefly describe a season in your life you could label as a growing pains season.

Video (15–20 minutes)

Play the Week 2 video segment. Invite participants to complete the Video Viewer Guide for Week 2 in the participant workbook as they watch (page 75).

Group Discussion (25–35 minutes, depending on session length)

Note: More material is provided than you will have time to include. Before the session, select what you want to cover, putting a check mark beside it in your book. Page references are provided for questions related to questions or activities in the participant workbook. For these questions, invite participants to share the answers they wrote in their books.

Video Discussion Questions
- When have you felt less than, undesirable, overlooked, or unchosen? How did that affect your understanding of God?
- Have you ever needed or wanted approval from someone and just never got it? What has that felt like?
- How was Leah able to praise God, even after feeling second best for so many years?
- Is it easy or difficult for you to believe that God sees you in your pain, that it is not hidden from Him?
- What does it mean to you that God is enough?

Participant Workbook Discussion Questions
1. When God pursues [Abram and Sarai] and invites them into partnership with His plans, they say yes. When God says, "Let's go!" they say, "Yes, Sir!" They didn't even know where they were headed! God just says, "Go to the land that I will show you," and they pack up and start walking! Surely, they had questions. Didn't Sarai have some fears about what lay ahead? Did they feel they were up to the task? (Day 1, page 46)

   - Read Genesis 12:1-4. What did God tell Abram and Sarai to do? What was their response? (page 46)
   - When have you made yourself fully available to God? What was the outcome? (page 46)
   - How have [your] fears affected your spiritual life? (page 44)

2. God does extraordinary things through ordinary people who put their trust in Him. . . . It's comforting to me that Abraham and Sarah were chosen for what appear to be simple reasons: availability and faithfulness. Our culture often chooses those who are good looking, charismatic, intelligent, wealthy, or talented. But God looks for different qualifications, and that is good news for us. Perhaps, being available and faithful sound ordinary and simple. But God often uses ordinary people in extraordinary ways when they respond to His pursuit of them. (Day 1, page 48)

- Which of the patriarchs and matriarchs of the faith do you connect with most when you look at the list from Hebrews 11? (see page 47)
- If this chapter were to be expanded to include *your* story, how would you hope it reads? (page 48)
- When is a time you have felt God calling and pursuing you? (page 48)

3. Scripture teaches us again and again that discipline is a sign of love. Note, however, that discipline and punishment are very different. Discipline is meant to correct a behavior. Punishment is meant to penalize. Perhaps, there are times for both, but discipline offered in love is the most effective means of maintaining a healthy relationship while offering correction. (Day 2, page 52)

- Read Revelation 3:19. What does it say about the connection between love and discipline? (page 52)
- Read Genesis 15:1-5 and Genesis 16:1-2. What was God's promise to Abram and Sarai? How did Abram and Sarai respond when it seemed like God had not kept His promise? (page 53)
- How would you describe the difference between discipline and punishment?

4. All God has to choose from is flawed people! Even when we make ourselves available and when we do our best to be faithful like Abraham and Sarah, we will not reach perfection this side of heaven. There will be times when we mess up. And like a good parent, there will be times when God disciplines us in order to refine our character. But even in our moments of redirection, we can know that God loves us relentlessly. (Day 2, pages 54–55)

- Would you say it's easy or difficult for you to trust God's instructions, even when you might have to wait for an answer?
- When have you taken matters into your own hands and thought you might know a better way than what God had in mind?
- How can Psalm 34:18 give us encouragement when we mess up?

5. It's interesting to me that bitterness is a noun. As I ponder that, it makes me imagine this emotion taking on a life of its own. Or perhaps invading a life where it steals all sweetness and replaces it with anger, disappointment, and resentment as the definition explains. (Day 3, page 59)

   - How did favoritism show up in the stories of Isaac and Ishmael, Jacob and Esau? Where do you see bitterness appear?
   - When have you experienced being the "favored one" in your family or friend group? When have you experienced being the opposite?
   - How have you known bitterness to "steal all sweetness" from your life?

6. We have the option to be released from bitterness if we so choose. (Day 3, page 59)

   - Do you agree that bitterness is a choice? Why or why not? How can we be released from any bitterness?
   - Read Hebrews 12:15 and Ephesians 4:31. What is the instruction in these verses? Is it really that simple to get rid of bitterness?
   - What work do you need to do to "get rid of all bitterness"? (page 60)

7. Like Leah and my friends from the second grade, I have had times in my life when I've known I was not the favorite. I was not the "chosen" one. Sometimes, it didn't matter to me one bit. Other times, it stung a lot! I imagine you have felt that way at times too. With maturity we can learn to be gracious and just move on with our lives. But, sometimes, no matter how hard we try to be mature, it just hurts. And, if we aren't careful, that hurt can turn to bitterness or anger, like it did with Esau and Leah. (Day 4, page 66)

   - Read Genesis 29:14-30. Who was the deceiver in this story? Who was chosen? Who was not chosen? (pages 64–65)

- Where do you see lying and deception as traits passed down generationally in this story?
- Which traits would you like to pass on to your children and grandchildren? Which ones do you want to stop with you? (page 66)

8. Recognizing who we are in Christ and knowing that our worth comes from Him, not from the approval of others, can lead us into lives free from bitterness and the hurt of not feeling chosen. In fact, we can move into a beautiful place of knowing our true worth and living into that value! (Day 4, page 66)

- Read 1 Peter 2:9. What does this verse say about you? How does this verse instruct us to live?
- What do you think it means to show others the goodness of God?
- What are some ways that we can let go of needing the approval of others and live confidently in the knowledge that we are chosen by the God of the universe?

9. "Character-building season" is a phrase reserved for times when you feel like you're losing repeatedly. I remember our friend saying, "God must be toughening you guys up for a big work in your future." Maybe so, because one thing was certain: We were not very tough at the time. Every criticism hurt. Every rejection stung. But with each setback, we began to toughen up. (Day 5, page 69)

- Read Genesis 37:3-4, 18, 23-28. What was the relationship between Joseph and his brothers? Why was there such animosity between them? What do you imagine Joseph was feeling as his brothers sold him into slavery? (page 70)
- What difficult seasons have you endured (death of a loved one, disease, job loss, depression, divorce, addiction, betrayal, etc.)? How are you different because of those experiences? (page 73)

10. Joseph redeems the trials he's been through by using what he's learned and the status he has achieved to bring good and not evil. His struggles were not wasted. This is known as redemptive suffering. And like God's passionate pursuit of His people, it is an overarching narrative of Scripture. God specializes in bringing good out of bad. (Day 5, page 72)

- Review your journaling pages on Day 5. How does God bring good from Joseph's years of struggle? (see pages 70–71)
- Read Romans 5:3. How is it that we can rejoice in seasons of problems and trials? How has God produced endurance in you through seasons of trial?
- How could God use your past struggles to minister to others?

11. God never wants to waste a hurt. He can turn your greatest suffering into your greatest ministry if you allow it. (page 73)

- What thoughts or discoveries are sticking with you from this week's study?

Deeper Conversation (15 minutes, for a 90-minute session)

Divide into smaller groups of two or three for deeper conversation. (Encourage the women to break into different groups each week.) Before the session, write on a marker board or chart paper the question or questions you want the groups to discuss:

- Have you had a character-building season in your life that led you to seek God with your whole heart? What does it mean to seek God with your whole heart? What are some ways that help you to connect with God?
- How have the struggles of your past made you who you are today? Would you trade them away? How has God made good from suffering in your life?

Closing Prayer (5 minutes)

Close the session by taking personal prayer requests from group members and leading the group in prayer. As you progress to later weeks in the study, you might encourage members to participate in the Closing Prayer by praying out loud for one another and the requests given.

Week 3

Pursued in a Cycle of Obedience and Rebellion

JUDGES, KINGS, AND PROPHETS

Leader Prep

Bible Story and Theme Overview

This week, our focus has been on a few of the judges, kings, and prophets of the Old Testament. Their stories are unique. The time frame spans hundreds of years. But what they have in common is that the God of the universe was passionate in wanting a relationship with each of them. God also wanted a relationship with His people, and He used these leaders to help guide the spiritual direction in the land. We also see that as they drift from Him, as humans often do, God is quick to respond when they turn their hearts back to Him. They are pursued—relentlessly!

Main Point

We all have highs and lows, and we need people, God's people, around us to help us remember that we are chosen, precious, and pursued—especially in our sad moments.

Key Scripture(s)

¹⁰Create in me a clean heart, O God.
    Renew a loyal spirit within me.
¹¹Do not banish me from your presence,
    and don't take your Holy Spirit from me.
¹²Restore to me the joy of your salvation,
    and make me willing to obey you.

                (Psalm 51:10-12)

If any of you lacks wisdom, you should ask God, who gives generously to all without finding fault, and it will be given to you.

                (James 1:5 NIV)

> [9]*Two are better than one,*
> *because they have a good return for their labor:*
> [10]*If either of them falls down,*
> *one can help the other up.*
> *But pity anyone who falls*
> *and has no one to help them up.*
> (Ecclesiastes 4:9-10 NIV)

What You Will Need

- *Pursued* DVD and DVD player, or equipment to stream the video online
- marker board or chart paper and markers
- stick-on name tags and markers (optional)
- iPod, smartphone, or tablet and portable speaker (optional)

Session Outline

Welcome and Opening Prayer (5–10 minutes, depending on session length)

To create a warm, welcoming environment as the women are gathering before the session begins, consider lighting one or more candles, providing coffee or other refreshments, or playing worship music, or all of these. (Bring an iPod, smartphone, or tablet and a portable speaker if desired.) Be sure to provide name tags if the women do not know one another or you have new participants in your group. Then, when you are ready to begin, pray the following prayer or offer your own:

Dear God, thank You for forgiving our rebellion time and time again. Thank You for Your grace and mercy that saves us and sets us right. Reveal Your heart to us as we study Your Word together. Amen.

Icebreaker (5 minutes)

Invite the women to share short, "popcorn" responses to the following question:

- Would you say you are more of a rule-follower or a rebel? Why?

Video (15–20 minutes)

Play the Week 3 video segment. Invite participants to complete the Video Viewer Guide for Week 3 in the participant workbook as they watch (page 107).

Group Discussion (25–35 minutes, depending on session length)

Note: More material is provided than you will have time to include. Before the session, select what you want to cover, putting a check mark beside it in your book. Page references are provided for questions related to questions or activities in the participant workbook. For these questions, invite participants to share the answers they wrote in their books.

Video Discussion Questions

- What is going on with the story of Hosea and Gomer? What does this relationship teach us about God's unconditional love?
- How could Hosea keep on forgiving?
- Why did Gomer keep on sinning?
- How has God pursued you despite your massive failures?

Participant Workbook Discussion Questions

1. When the people of Israel stay close to God and His instructions under the judge's leadership, the nation does well. But, when they deviate from God's direction, they fall into trouble (a universal truth for us all, by the way)....The last of the judges is Samuel. During his leadership, the people of Israel took a look around at neighboring countries and decided that they no longer wanted to be led by God and His representatives, the judges. Instead, they wanted what they saw others in the world had—a king. God's people shifted their focus from spiritual to earthly leadership. (Day 1, page 79)

   - When in your lifetime, or in history, have you seen or heard about the church deviating from God's guidance and embracing cultural norms instead? (page 80)
   - Why do you think Israel wanted an earthly king?
   - When and how have your earthly desires gotten you into trouble? (page 81)

2. In our theme of being pursued, it is important to note that although the nation rejects God's appointed leaders, the judges, and seeks an earthly king, God does not abandon them. Instead, He gives them the desire of their hearts, an earthly king, and then allows them to reap the consequences of that choice. But, as a loving Father, He never goes far. And when they get into enough trouble, and they do, they turn back to Him. The great news is as the Great Pursuer, God

stands ready to help you, no matter what you've done or how far you've drifted. All you have to do is turn to Him. He is standing there with arms wide open. (Day 1, pages 81–82)

- Why does God sometimes let us have our way and let us face the consequences? Do you have an example from your own life?
- In what ways do you struggle to be obedient to God? How have you experienced God's love and kindness in those moments?
- Read Romans 7:15-20. What is Paul getting at? Why is obedience to God such a struggle sometimes? How does this passage feel true in your life?

3. When we think of David, so many images come to mind: shepherd, poet, musician, king, and ancestor of Jesus. These are all correct, and they are strong and faithful descriptions. But to capture the full picture, there is another list: betrayer, adulterer, murderer, and liar. Scripture makes no attempt to hide David's imperfections. Second Samuel 11 gives us great detail about David's less than righteous actions. (Day 2, page 86)

- Read 2 Samuel 11:1-5. What was the result of David and Bathsheba's encounter? (page 86)
- Read 2 Samuel 11:6-17. What was the end result of David's actions? (page 86)
- Read Acts 13:22. How does the writer describe David? (page 87) How is it that a man who covers his infidelity with murder is described as a man after God's own heart?

4. David was more than remorseful for what he had done. He was repentant. There is a huge difference between the two. Remorse is an emotion—being sorry for one's sin. But repentance is an action, a turning away from that sin. David was repentant. (Day 2, page 88)

- In your own words, describe the difference between being repentant and being remorseful.
- Read Psalm 51. What did David want from God? (page 87) What is the prayer of David's heart?
- What do you imagine God might have felt as He heard David repent in this passionate way?

- How did David's response to his sin shape his legacy? How does your response to your own sin shape both your legacy and your relationship with God?

5. Intelligence and wisdom are very different things. A person can be very knowledgeable in various areas—travel, technology, culinary arts, astronomy, science, mathematics, even theology—but that will not guarantee wisdom. The good news is God loves and pursues all people, whether or not they are wise. But the benefits of wisdom are much greater than intelligence alone! (Day 3, page 91)

   - How would you describe the difference between intelligence and wisdom?
   - How does a person become wise?
   - What reason does Proverbs 13:20 give for seeking wisdom? (page 91)

6. There is a huge disparity between knowing what is wise and doing what is wise. King Solomon is a great example of this. Although, through God's grace, he was the wisest person who had ever lived (1 Kings 4:30), he often did not make wise choices. Instead of pursuing God's purposes for himself and the kingdom, Solomon regularly pursued his own pleasures. (Day 3, page 92)

   - Read Romans 7:15-20. How do these passages apply to your life today? (page 93)
   - How is closeness to God connected to our depth of wisdom?
   - Read James 1:5. What does this passage say about gaining wisdom? How can you seek wisdom and living such that you know what is wise and then do what is wise?

7. My friendships with other believers encourage my faith. They make me laugh, hold me accountable, and give me an outlet to share dreams, thoughts, and ideas. They pray with me and for me, and I do the same for them. Life without them is harder and not as much fun. (Day 4, pages 96–97)

   - How do your believing friends encourage your faith and help you to grow both as a person and in faith?
   - How has living through a pandemic affected your friendships? How have you stayed connected even when isolated?

8. We need people like Elisha in our lives—other Christ followers who love the Lord and who can come alongside us, freely speaking into our lives to remind us who and whose we are. We are not meant to do life alone. We all have highs and lows, and we need people—God's people—around us to help us remember that we are chosen, precious, and pursued—especially in our sad moments. (Day 4, page 100)

    - Read Ecclesiastes 4:9-10. According to these verses, why do we need one another? When have you been helped by a fellow believer? (page 100)
    - Read 1 Kings 19:19-21. Whom does God provide as a companion? How do you think Elijah might have felt in having a ministry partner? (page 99)
    - Have you ever felt a sense of being on a spiritual roller coaster—one minute flying high with God and the next minute terribly lonely or depressed? What was that like for you? How did friends help you in that season?

9. We need to ask God to surround us with mature believers from whom we can learn. We need to be aware that there are those out there who need to learn from us. And we need to run to these opportunities. (Day 5, page 105)

    - Who has been a mentor for you? (page 104)
    - Read 2 Kings 2:1-2, 9-11. What do these verses tell us about this friendship? (page 104)
    - Read Titus 2:3-5. How can you put this passage into action?

10. As we mature, we should return the favor by allowing others to stand on our shoulders. Sharing the wisdom we have learned from the Lord, His Word, and from our own mistakes is a valuable gift to the next generation. Our pouring into other people—and their pouring into us—is another way in which God pursues His children. (Day 5, pages 105–106)

    - How can you serve others as a mentor? What strengths of character or skills do you have that you could share with the next generation? (page 106)
    - What did you learn about mentorship from Elisha in your readings this week?
    - How does God pursue us through mentoring friendships?

11. As a woman who is being relentlessly pursued by your heavenly Father, you can be assured that God wants you to have strong, faithful relationships. God plays a part in this and you have a role to play. (Day 5, page 105)

- What thoughts or discoveries are sticking with you from this week's study?

Deeper Conversation (15 minutes, for a 90-minute session)

Divide into smaller groups of two or three for deeper conversation. (Encourage the women to break into different groups each week.) Before the session, write on a marker board or chart paper the question or questions you want the groups to discuss:

- What growing pains have you had in your walk with God? When have you fallen into traps? How did God rescue you at just the right time?
- How have you gained wisdom from those growing pains?

Give a two-minute warning before time is up so that the groups may wrap up their discussion.

Closing Prayer (5 minutes)

Close the session by taking personal prayer requests from group members and leading the group in prayer. Encourage members to participate in the Closing Prayer by praying out loud for one another and the requests given.

Pursued and Rescued

JESUS

Leader Prep

Bible Story and Theme Overview

This week we have considered how God relentlessly pursues us, focusing on the ultimate way this is expressed—through the life, death, and resurrection of Jesus. Jesus came to lead the search for those who are lost. He came to lead the search for you and for me!

Main Point

We are the reason Jesus came to earth on a rescue mission.

Key Scripture(s)

⁶*You see, at just the right time, when we were still powerless, Christ died for the ungodly.* ⁷*Very rarely will anyone die for a righteous person, though for a good person someone might possibly dare to die.* ⁸*But God demonstrates his own love for us in this: While we were still sinners, Christ died for us.*

(Romans 5:6-8 NIV)

⁹*This is how God showed his love among us: He sent his one and only Son into the world that we might live through him.* ¹⁰*This is love; not that we loved God, but that he loved us and sent his Son as an atoning sacrifice for our sins.* ¹¹*Dear friends, since God so loved us, we also ought to love one another.*

(1 John 4:9-11 NIV)

²⁵*Husbands, love your wives, as Christ loved the church and gave himself up for her,* ²⁶*that he might sanctify her, having cleansed her by the washing of water with the word,* ²⁷*so that he might present the church to himself in splendor, without spot or wrinkle or any such thing, that she might be holy and without blemish.*

(Ephesians 5:25-27 ESV)

My dear children, I write this to you so that you will not sin. But if anybody does sin, we have an advocate with the Father—Jesus Christ, the Righteous One.

(1 John 2:1 NIV)

What You Will Need

- *Pursued* DVD and DVD player, or equipment to stream the video online
- marker board or chart paper and markers
- stick-on name tags and markers (optional)
- iPod, smartphone, or tablet and portable speaker (optional)

Session Outline

Welcome and Opening Prayer (5–10 minutes, depending on session length)

To create a warm, welcoming environment as the women are gathering before the session begins, consider lighting one or more candles, providing coffee or other refreshments, or playing worship music, or all of these. (Bring an iPod, smartphone, or tablet and a portable speaker if desired.) Be sure to provide name tags if the women do not know one another or you have new participants in your group. Then, when you are ready to begin, pray the following prayer or offer your own:

Dear God, thank You for Jesus, our Rescuer. Thank You that You never leave us or turn Your back on us. You chase after us and even sent Your own Son to save us. Thank You. May we feel Your presence with us as we study Your Word. Amen.

Icebreaker (5 minutes)

Invite the women to share short, "popcorn" responses to the following question:

- Recall a time when something precious to you was lost. How did you feel?

Video (15–20 minutes)

Play the Week 4 video segment. Invite participants to complete the Video Viewer Guide for Week 4 in the participant workbook as they watch. (page 135)

Group Discussion (25–35 minutes, depending on session length)

Note: More material is provided than you will have time to include. Before the session, select what you want to cover, putting a check mark beside it in your book. Page references are provided for questions related to questions or activities in the participant workbook. For these questions, invite participants to share the answers they wrote in their books.

Video Discussion Questions

- When was the last time you had to adjust major plans and move forward in a new way? Was "Plan B" a success or a failure?
- Even knowing that a sacrifice would be required, God still created us, chose us, and pursued us! How would you describe that kind of love?
- What do you take delight in?
- How does it feel to know that God takes delight in you?

Participant Workbook Discussion Questions

1. The lost sheep, coin, and sons of Luke 15 are among the best-known parables in Scripture. They illustrate beautifully the lengths God will go to in order to rescue those who are lost. (Day 1, page 112)

    - Review the stories of the lost sheep, coin, and sons in Luke 15. What do you think Jesus is getting at with these stories?
    - When have you felt lost or separated from God? What brought you back?

2. I had always read the story of the sheep and thought, *Okay, cool story. Jesus really loves people far from Him. He even goes after them. He loves them so much. But, I am a church kid. I grew up in Sunday school, youth group, the whole deal. So I guess I'm just one of the ninety-nine....* As I was reading this story again.... God spoke to my heart and said, "No ma'am, you are not number seventy-four out of ninety-nine. You are the One. You are the One I would look high and low for. You are the One Jesus went to the cross for. You are the One, Jennifer, and so is every person you will ever meet." (Day 1, page 113)

    - Have you ever considered yourself as the *One*? What does it mean to you that Jesus would look high and low for you?

- Read Luke 19:10. How do you understand what Jesus means by "to seek and to save the lost"? What does this mean for you personally? (page 114)
- Read Romans 6:23. Why do we need Jesus to rescue us? What does this mean for you personally? (page 114)

3. In wanting to save ourselves and control our own circumstances, we may often fight against the very One who wants to and has the power to rescue us. (Day 2, page 117)

- When have you struggled to solve a problem on your own, only to find that once you released it to God, He was there waiting to rescue you? What lessons did you learn in that situation? (page 117)
- Read Psalm 49:7-8a. What are some ways that people try to pull themselves up by their own bootstraps? (page 118)
- Have you struggled with the fact that you can't save yourself or that you can't work your way to salvation? If so, describe that struggle.

4. God knew we were drowning in our own sins. Humanity needed a Savior. This is why Jesus came to earth. He came on a rescue mission. If there had been another way for us to be made right with God, surely Jesus would not have had to take on human flesh and endure the cross. But Scripture tells us that He willingly did this so that we could be saved. (Day 2, page 118)

- Read Hebrews 12:2b. What was the source of the joy set before Jesus? (page 118)
- Would you rather struggle to survive or surrender to rescue? When have you had seasons of struggle? When have you had seasons of surrender?

5. The intricacies of God's nature are complex, but the message of how He feels about you is not. It's simple: You are loved. Passionately, relentlessly, in a way that may make no sense at all. God loves you! Scriptures promise us that again and again. (Day 3, page 121)

- Read Isaiah 54:10 and 1 John 3:1. What do these verses say about God's love for you? Share your own expression of these words. (pages 121–122)
- How did you come to know God's love for you?

6. Far too many people have a distorted image of God. Perhaps, they see Him as an unpleasant parent or strict disciplinarian just waiting to pounce. This faulty image may lead them to distance themselves from God and His purpose for their lives. (Day 3, pages 122–123)

   - Read 1 John 3:1. How would you say this verse in your own words? (pages 120–121)
   - What has your image of God been in the past? How does it compare to the description of God in this verse? (pages 120–121)
   - What are the traits of a good parent? How do those traits apply to how God pursues you? (page 123)

7. The betrothal process doesn't sound like romance as we know it today, but it was a beautiful process honored for hundreds of years. It represented dedication, love, and commitment. The faithful bridegroom went ahead of his wife to prepare a permanent home for her. When the time was right, he went to bring her home, where he promised to care for her and make her part of his family forevermore. . . . This is the context in which the people of Jesus's audience were living. So, when He tells them in John 14 that He is going to prepare a room for them, it is familiar language. (Day 4, page 127)

   - Read John 14:1-3. What actions does Jesus promise to take on your behalf? What does Jesus ask you to do? (page 127)
   - Read Ephesians 5:25-27. How does Paul describe the relationship between Christ and the church? (page 128)
   - Think about the level of intimacy between husband and wife. How do you feel as you think about that level of intimacy in your relationship with Jesus? (page 128)

8. Scripture gives us glimpses of the beauty and majesty of our eternal home. Streets of gold, rivers like crystals, no sadness, no sickness, worship and joy are the norm. (Day 5, page 130)

   - How do you imagine the moment when you will stand before God face-to-face? (page 131)
   - What do you think of when you consider what heaven will be like?
   - Who will you run to find there after that first encounter with Jesus face-to-face?

9. You are a daughter of the Creator of the universe. Chosen, pursued, and loved.
    That is your blessed assurance. Jesus is yours. And you belong to Him.
    (Day 5, page 134)

    - Read Romans 8:31-39. What questions does Paul ask in these verses?
      What answers would you give in response? (pages 132–133)
    - Read 1 John 2:1. What does it mean that Jesus is an advocate? How would you
      describe that role? (page 133)
    - Read Hebrews 7:25. Knowing that Jesus stands ready to serve as your Advocate,
      how can you walk more boldly in your faith? (page 134)

10. Rather than condemn us, Jesus intercedes for us. He bridges the gap. (page 133)

    - What thoughts or discoveries are sticking with you from this week's study?

Deeper Conversation (15 minutes, for a 90-minute session)

Divide into smaller groups of two or three for deeper conversation. (Encourage the women to break into different groups each week.) Before the session, write on a marker board or chart paper the question or questions you want the groups to discuss:

- How would you tell someone about their need for Jesus? Discuss some ways to share His love with others—with words and with actions. Tell about a time when you had success in sharing Jesus. Tell about a time when it didn't go so well.

Give a two-minute warning before time is up so that the groups may wrap up their discussion.

Closing Prayer (5 minutes)

Close the session by taking personal prayer requests from group members and leading the group in prayer. Encourage members to participate in the Closing Prayer by praying out loud for one another and the requests given.

Week 5

Pursued in Our Unsavory Moments

NEW TESTAMENT ENCOUNTERS

Leader Prep

Bible Story and Theme Overview

This week, we focused on encounters in the New Testament where Jesus pursues with passion unlikely candidates for His attention. Unsavory, rough, sinful, despised, even cruel—all words that could describe the cast of this week's devotional lessons. Their stories vary greatly, yet they have one thing in common: God's Son sought them out in order to offer them love, hope, and new life in Him. He chose to be in relationship with each of them.

Main Point

We are the unsavory, rough, sinful, despised—and perhaps even cruel at times. Yet Jesus pursues us!

Key Scriptures

As Jesus was going on down the road, he saw a tax collector, Matthew, sitting at a tax collection booth. "Come and be my disciple," Jesus said to him, and Matthew jumped up and went along with him.

(Matthew 9:9 TLB)

18As Jesus was walking beside the Sea of Galilee, he saw two brothers, Simon called Peter and his brother Andrew. They were casting a net into the lake, for they were fishermen. 19"Come, follow me," Jesus said, "and I will send you out to fish for people." 20At once they left their nets and followed him.

21Going on from there, he saw two other brothers, James son of Zebedee and his brother John. They were in a boat with their father Zebedee, preparing their nets. Jesus called them, 22and immediately they left the boat and their father and followed him.

(Matthew 4:18-22 NIV)

As far as the east is from the west,
so far has he removed our transgressions from us.
(Psalm 103:12 NIV)

What You Will Need

- *Pursued* DVD and DVD player, or equipment to stream the video online
- marker board or chart paper and markers
- stick-on name tags and markers (optional)
- iPod, smartphone, or tablet and portable speaker (optional)

Session Outline

Welcome and Opening Prayer (5–10 minutes, depending on session length)

To create a warm, welcoming environment as the women are gathering before the session begins, consider lighting one or more candles, providing coffee or other refreshments, or playing worship music, or all of these. (Bring an iPod, smartphone, or tablet and a portable speaker if desired.) Be sure to provide name tags if the women do not know one another or you have new participants in your group. Then, when you are ready to begin, pray the following prayer or offer your own:

Dear God, thank You for loving us in our less-than-faithful moments. You are kind and good and merciful. You meet us again and again with grace and tenderness. Help us to choose You first, to seek You above everything else, and to make You the center of our lives. Help us to hear You as we study Your Word. Amen.

Icebreaker (5 minutes)

Invite the women to share short, "popcorn" responses to the following question:

- What would you say are the top three blessings in your life? (Name the first things that come to mind.)

Video (15–20 minutes)

Play the Week 5 video segment. Invite participants to complete the Video Viewer Guide for Week 5 in the participant workbook as they watch. (page 170)

Group Discussion (25–35 minutes, depending on session length)

Note: More material is provided than you will have time to include. Before the session, select what you want to cover, putting a check mark beside it in your book. Page references are provided for questions related to questions or activities in the participant workbook. For these questions, invite participants to share the answers they wrote in their books.

Video Discussion Questions

- Imagine Jesus showing up at your worst moment. Are you relieved He's there or afraid of what's coming?
- What do Jesus's words and actions in the story of the woman caught in adultery teach us about how Jesus meets us in our worst moments?
- What is the path to heaven?
- How do we make the journey to salvation too complex sometimes?
- Have you ever struggled to believe Jesus would forgive you? If so, how did Jesus convince you of His love?

Participant Workbook Discussion Questions

1. Matthew surely fit [the description of a crooked tax collector]. Yet Jesus called him. What a shock that must have been to those in the crowd. Even the disciples must have murmured. But, surely the one most shocked must have been Matthew himself. (Day 1, page 140)

   - When have you been surprised at who God uses?
   - Read Matthew 9:9-13. Which of the characters in the story are you most like? Why? (page 141)
   - What is at the heart of what Jesus is doing and saying in this story? What does it say about His purpose on earth?

2. Matthew not only responds personally to Jesus but He also wants to give his friends the same opportunity. So, he holds a dinner party for scoundrels. Some translations call them "tax collectors and sinners" (NIV). The Message calls them "crooks and riffraff." Sounds like a tough crowd. Matthew experienced the joy of being chosen and he wants to share that with those he knows. It doesn't seem to cross his mind that anyone would be too rough or rotten to sit at the table with Jesus. (Day 1, Page 142)

- When have you been like Matthew, responding immediately to God's prompting? (page 141)
- When have you hesitated to respond faithfully? (page 141)
- What are some ways you can invite others to follow Jesus with you?

3. As we follow the progression of Peter, Andrew, James, and John, we see evidence of how they grow in maturity and in the fruits of the Spirit. Peter, for example, is quick with a sword to defend Jesus when He is arrested. However, after the Resurrection Peter lays down the sword and is quick to respond with the message of salvation instead of violence. As a result, instead of a soldier with a severed ear, we see thousands come to Christ through Peter's messages. He has grown to not only know the message of Jesus, but to embody His character. This is the goal of a mature disciple. (Day 2, page 146)

- Read Philippians 2:1-11. What does this passage tell us about Jesus? What instructions are we given? (page 147)
- Read Matthew 4:18-22. What did these disciples do when they heard Jesus call them? (page 145)
- What do you think might have been on their mind as they fished? What do you think they imagined when Jesus told them they could "fish for people"?

4. In this world where we can follow people on social media, or follow someone's career path, or follow their rise to stardom, it's easy to confuse information with relationships. A disciple goes much deeper than surface-level imitation. A disciple becomes an imitator of the one he or she follows, trying to live into the values of the one he or she follows. (Day 2, page 148)

- Read 1 John 2:6. In what areas of life do you feel you are walking in the way in which Jesus did? (page 148)
- Read Ephesians 5:1. What would it look like for you to imitate God in the following areas: at home, at work, with your family, at church, in a difficult relationship? (pages 148–149)
- What is the danger of placing people on a pedestal?

5. Second Corinthians 5:17 tells us that "anyone who belongs to Christ has become a new person. The old life is gone; a new life has begun!" This is the

promise to all who come to know and trust Jesus with their lives. As we discover the love of Christ, it transforms us into new creations, revealing the character that God intended us to have from our birth. And Jesus proclaimed that this new life comes through Him (John 14:6). (Day 3, page 152)

- When have you needed a fresh start?
- How have you felt God's cleansing in the past?
- Read John 8:1-11. What do you see, hear, smell, taste, and touch in this passage? (page 152)

6. The love and forgiveness of God is so deep and rich. . . . God yearns for us to find recovered and restored lives through Him. "As far as east is from the west" and "as clean as freshly fallen snow"—the writers used these metaphors to help us understand that we are washed completely when we turn from sin and embrace God. (Day 3, page 154)

- Read Psalm 103:12. What does this mean to you?
- What are some other metaphors you can think of to describe God's grace and love?
- How would you imagine the next part of the story for the woman caught in adultery? What does her life look like one year later?

7. There's more to forgiveness than just wanting to be forgiven ourselves. As believers, we are to take on the likeness of Christ. (Day 4, page 158)

- Read Ephesians 4:32 and Matthew 6:15. What do these verses say about our call to be like Jesus?
- Whom have you struggled to forgive? What feelings come to the surface when you think of them? (Share only the feelings, not the person's name.) Whose forgiveness have you received in the past? Which do you think more about— those you have forgiven or those who have forgiven you? (page 158)
- Which do you think is harder—to forgive or to be forgiven? Why?
- When and where have you seen God miraculously show up in your life in the past?

8. Jesus knew that Peter's worst and best days lay ahead of him. His faith and ministry were stronger after his denial than they had ever been. As we see

Peter preach and lead the church in the Book of Acts, he is no longer cowering or denying Jesus. Instead, he is proclaiming Christ crucified and resurrected boldly and publicly. Something has changed. When Jesus restores Peter during breakfast by the sea, He sends him off with a new sense of purpose, forgiven and clean. (Day 4, page 161)

- Read Matthew 26:33-35, 69-75. How does the story of Peter's denial demonstrate the depth of Jesus's love for us?
- Read John 21:1-17. Put yourself in the story as if you were Peter. What are you feeling during this interaction? (page 160)
- What does Peter's story teach us about the path of discipleship?
- What does Peter's story teach us about Jesus's willingness to pursue us at all cost?

9. Upon hearing that His dear friend Lazarus is sick, Jesus tells the disciples that He is headed back to Judea. During their last visit to the Jerusalem region, some of the Jews had tried to stone Jesus, so the disciples discouraged Jesus from returning there. But Thomas bravely speaks up in John 11:16 and says, "Let's go, too—and die with Jesus." Thomas knows that heading back into Judea may be a death sentence for them all, but he is ready to go when Jesus commands. (Day 5, pages 165–166)

- When have you faced real danger for following Jesus? When have you suffered for your faith? How did you handle it? (page 166)
- Would you say that following Jesus is a safe path or a path that requires bravery? Why?

10. Jesus can handle our questions. In fact, as we seek Him, we find that He meets us in our search. This is not a game of hide-and-go-seek where the hider doesn't want to be found. When we search for Jesus and when we come to Him with our questions, we actually find that He was already pursuing us. (Day 5, page 168)

- Read John 20:24-29. Why do you think Thomas refused to believe his friends? (page 167)
- Read Jeremiah 29:13 and Matthew 7:7. What do these verses teach us about God's attitude toward us? (page 168)

- Thomas had doubts and questions. What questions do you have for God? What doubts have you had? How have those doubts affected your faith journey? (page 168)

11. At the end of Thomas's interaction with Jesus in John 20, did you notice that you are mentioned? You are! Look again. Jesus says, "You believe because you have seen me. Blessed are those who believe without seeing me" (John 20:29). You and I are "those" people Jesus was talking about here—the ones who believe without physically encountering Jesus. (page 169)

- What thoughts or discoveries are sticking with you from this week's study?

Deeper Conversation (15 minutes, for a 90-minute session)

Divide into smaller groups of two or three for deeper conversation. (Encourage the women to break into different groups each week.) Before the session, write on a marker board or chart paper the question or questions you want the groups to discuss:

- Disciples need time to become covered in the dust of their rabbi, but time will not create a solid coating of dust unless the disciple is following closely. What would it mean for you to be covered in the dust of your rabbi Jesus? What are some intentional practices you do now or could begin in order to get closer to Jesus, learn from Him, and imitate Him?

Give a two-minute warning before time is up so that the groups may wrap up their discussion.

Closing Prayer (5 minutes)

Close the session by taking personal prayer requests from group members and leading the group in prayer. Encourage members to participate in the Closing Prayer by praying out loud for one another and the requests given.

Week 6

Pursued for the Sake of Others

PARTICIPATING IN GOD'S RESCUE MISSION

Leader Prep

Bible Story and Theme Overview

This week we've seen that once we come to know Jesus, the pursuit is not over. Instead, we are invited to join God in pursuing others with His love and message. We are part of God's chosen family, and being part of the family means we inherit the work of the family business—sharing love through Christ.

Main Point

Our primary goal as believers is to love God and love others in real and practical ways, ways that point them to Jesus.

Key Scriptures

[19]"Go and make disciples of all nations, baptizing them in the name of the Father and of the Son and of the Holy Spirit, [20]and teaching them to obey everything I have commanded you. And surely I am with you always, to the very end of the age."

(Matthew 28:19-20 NIV)

But in your hearts revere Christ as Lord. Always be prepared to give an answer to everyone who asks you to give the reason for the hope that you have. But do this with gentleness and respect.

(1 Peter 3:15 NIV)

Many of the Samaritans from that town believed in him because of the woman's testimony.

(John 4:39 NIV)

[6]When we were utterly helpless, Christ came at just the right time and died for us sinners. [7]Now, most people would not be willing to die for an upright person, though someone might perhaps be willing to die for a person who is especially good. [8]But God showed His great love for us by sending Christ to die for us while we were still sinners. [9]And since we have been made right in God's sight by the blood of Christ, he will certainly save us from God's condemnation. [10]For since our friendship

with God was restored by the death of his Son while we were still his enemies, we will certainly be saved through the life of his Son. ¹¹So now we can rejoice in our wonderful new relationship with God because our Lord Jesus Christ has made us friends of God.

(Romans 5:6-11)

What You Will Need

- *Pursued* DVD and DVD player, or equipment to stream the video online
- marker board or chart paper and markers
- stick-on name tags and markers (optional)
- iPod, smartphone, or tablet and portable speaker (optional)

Session Outline

Welcome and Opening Prayer (5–10 minutes, depending on session length)

To create a warm, welcoming environment as the women are gathering before the session begins, consider lighting one or more candles, providing coffee or other refreshments, or playing worship music, or all of these. (Bring an iPod, smartphone, or tablet and a portable speaker if desired.) Be sure to provide name tags if the women do not know one another or you have new participants in your group. Then, when you are ready to begin, pray the following prayer or offer your own:

Dear God, thank You for inviting us into Your rescuing effort. Give us strength and courage to say yes when You call us. Thank You for saving us and for sending us. Open our eyes, ears, and hearts as we study Your Word. Amen.

Icebreaker (5 minutes)

Invite the women to share short, "popcorn" responses to the following question:

- What is one way you can share your passion about Jesus with others?

Video (15–20 minutes)

Play the Week 6 video segment. Invite participants to complete the Video Viewer Guide for Week 6 in the participant workbook as they watch (page 201).

Group Discussion (25–35 minutes, depending on session length)

Note: More material is provided than you will have time to include. Before the session, select what you want to cover, putting a check mark beside it in your book. Page references are provided for questions related to questions or activities in the participant workbook. For these questions, invite participants to share the answers they wrote in their books.

Video Discussion Questions

- What does it mean to be a show-and-tell believer?
- What are some ways to tell people about Jesus—with your words and with your actions?
- Have you ever spent time getting ready to share your faith—preparing your elevator speech and praying for opportunities? What was the result of your preparation?
- What is your elevator speech to tell others about Jesus?
- How could you engage when you see someone hurting? How might this be an opportunity to offer Jesus?
- Are you ready to call yourself a "pursued pursuer" yet? Why or why not?

Participant Workbook Discussion Questions

1. As His followers, Jesus commissions us to share that passion [about restoring what is lost]. As His children, we are to take on the family business of loving people and sharing the message of Christ with everyone everywhere. While on earth, Jesus leaves us with clear instructions. We, His disciples, are to continue the rescue mission. (Day 1, page 174)

   - Read Matthew 28:19-20. What is this passage called? Who followed the Great Commission by telling you about Jesus? (page 175)
   - Have you ever told someone else about Jesus's love and forgiveness? If so, what was that experience like? (page 175)

2. God is passionate about pursuing all people and asks you to become part of that pursuit. Figuring out how to do that can be tricky. We don't want to be so aggressive that we alienate people. And, we don't want to be so passionate that we come off as kooks. Because we don't want to offend anyone, embarrass

ourselves, and, sometimes, because we just don't know quite what to do, we often do nothing. But we can and must tell others about Jesus in real and life-changing ways. (Day 1, page 176)

- When have you struggled to share about Jesus but also worried about offending or alienating people?
- What are some ways to live out the Great Commission without overdoing it or underdoing it?
- Read Romans 10:9-14. According to Paul, how can a person be saved? Who has the opportunity to do this? What dilemma does Paul present? (page 177)

3. We didn't mean to drift, but we did. Without realizing it, we had become so occupied with the care and discipleship of those inside the church that we had begun to neglect the work of reaching out to those in our community who had not yet found God relevant in their lives. It took an intentional effort to shift our focus back to reaching people far from God. Unless we're intentional, we all tend to drift. (Day 2, page 180)

- Have you drifted from the Great Commission—the command to make disciples in Matthew 28:19-20? If so, how do you think that drift began? (page 181)
- Who is your One? [Who are you praying for and believing for?] (page 181)
- How have you reached out to your One in the past? Has it been effective? If not, what barriers have you faced? (page 181)

4. A popular saying in churches today is "Found people find people." Another way of saying that could be "Pursued people pursue people." Both phrases encourage the same goal: we who have come to know the love of Jesus need to help others find it, too. (Day 2, page 184)

- What does it mean that "found people find people" or "pursued people pursue people"?
- Read John 1:45-46. What was Nathanael's approach for telling people about Jesus? How did he respond to opposition? (page 184)
- What are some ways to make sure we're not always surrounded only by believers? Where can we go to tell others about Jesus?

5. Our primary goal as believers is to love God and love others in real and practical ways, ways that point them to Jesus. It doesn't get much more practical than helping people find the love and eternal security found in Christ. (Day 3, page 187)

    • Read John 4:1-18. What was so unusual about this encounter? How did Jesus turn the conversation toward religious things? (page 188)
    • What does this story teach us about living out the Great Commission?
    • Read John 4:28, 39. What did the woman do? How did her testimony change lives?

6. God was so consumed with passion for us that He sent Jesus to earth to pursue us. In return He wants us to pursue others. I am one of the redeemed. If you are too, then it's our responsibility to share Jesus with those around us. But we often run into a problem when it comes to sharing our faith. Sometimes, our passion for the lost turns cold. (Day 4, page 193)

    • Who does your heart break for? (page 192)
    • Read Colossians 4:5-6 and Romans 12:9-11. How can you best live out these passages? (page 193)
    • Would you say that your passion for the lost wanes at times? If so, why do you think that is?

7. As we learn to rest in knowing that we are loved and pursued by our heavenly Father, it frees us to offer that love in great big doses to those around us. We can take our eyes off of ourselves and focus on the needs of others. The more we receive what God has done for us, the more likely we are to share it with those so desperately in need of Him. (Day 4, page 195)

    • Read Revelation 2:3-4. In these verses, what does it mean to lose your "first love"?
    • Read Revelation 3:15-16. How is the church described? Why would being cold toward the things of God be better than being lukewarm? (page 194)
    • Would you say you are cold or lukewarm right now in your passion to reach others with the love of Jesus? How can you grow you passion for the lost?

8. The meta-narrative (overall story) from Genesis to Revelation remains constant. God's love for His people is relentless. Although the settings and characters change with each generation, the theme of every book of the Bible is amazingly the same: God passionately pursues His people. In fact, He is so passionate in His pursuit that when it would appear we are beyond reach, He creates a new way for us to be reconciled to Him. (Day 5, page 198)

   • How would you tell the overarching story of the Bible in just a few sentences?
   • Read Romans 5:6-11. Describe life without Jesus and life with Jesus. (page 198)
   • Read Mark 16:15. How will you join God in pursuing those far from Him? (page 199)

9. You are desired, loved, and pursued by the One who knows you best. God's love for you is absolutely relentless! When the voices of this world crowd in, let this be the message you hear most clearly: The God of the universe passionately pursues you! (Day 5, page 200)

   • Have you ever doubted that you are desired, loved, and pursued by God? If so, how did God break through to change your mind?
   • How do the voices of this world crowd in and drown out the voice of truth?
   • What does it mean that God's love is relentless? How does that change the way you live your life?

10. We are part of God's chosen family, and being part of the family means we inherit the work of the family business—sharing love through Christ. (Day 5, page 199)

    • What thoughts or discoveries are sticking with you from studying about God's relentless pursuit of your heart?

Deeper Conversation (15 minutes, for a 90-minute session)

Divide into smaller groups of two or three for deeper conversation. (Encourage the women to break into different groups each week.) Before the session, write on a marker board or chart paper the question or questions you want the groups to discuss:

- If you had the opportunity to share Christ in less than three minutes, how would you do it? What would you do and say?
- Recall a few highs and lows of your spiritual life, noting the specific ways you now can see that God was pursuing you. (page 198)

Give a two-minute warning before time is up so that the groups may wrap up their discussion.

Closing Prayer (5 minutes)

Close the session by taking personal prayer requests from group members and leading the group in prayer. Encourage members to participate in the Closing Prayer by praying out loud for one another and the requests given, and invite them to continue praying for one another in the weeks to come.

Video Viewer Guide
Answers

Week 1
give up

pursues

passionately loves

Week 2
sees

pursues

enough

Week 3
love / forgiveness

commands

committed

failures

Week 4
rescue mission

price / life

sacrifice / time

delights

Week 5
simple

available

deeds

Week 6
come / see

show / tell

ready

elevator story

opportunities

engage

Printed in the USA
CPSIA information can be obtained
at www.ICGtesting.com
LVHW081949310124
770290LV00004B/9